5A

Student Workbook

Five A

by Barbara A. Wilson

READING SYSTEM

READING SYSTEM

STUDENT WORKBOOK FIVE A

THIRD EDITION

by Barbara A. Wilson

Wilson Language Training
175 West Main Street
Millbury, Massachusetts 01527-1441
(508) 865-5699

ISBN 1-56778-086-5	Student Workbook Five A	Item# SW5A
ISBN 1-56778-080-6	Student Workbooks 1-6 A	Item# WRW16A
ISBN 1-56778-079-2	Student Workbooks 1-12 A	Item# WRW12 A

The Wilson Reading System is published by:

Wilson Language Training Corp.
175 West Main Street
Millbury, MA 01527-1441

Printed in the U.S.A.

Read the words. Underline and mark the syllable: c = closed; v-e = vowel-consonant-e; o = open. Mark the vowels. e.g. crȳ
o

cry	flu	hope
pro	hide	sky
plug	be	so
shy	brake	melt
shelf	fry	by
no	sly	try
swim	go	fill
fly	I	he
bike	pine	shine
lost	me	help

Read the nonsense words. Underline and mark the syllable: c = closed; e = v-c-e; o = open. Mark the vowels.

ne	plib	thren
pute	bli	threne
shipe	blipe	plo
cho	pru	stome
chot	spone	cret
plit	ste	slabe
bri	vome	gly
grome	quo	glip
mupe	shene	chy
zan	bla	scret

Read the sentence. Select the correct word from the box to complete the sentence. Write the word on the line. Reread the completed sentence. Use each word in the box only once.

sly	cry	by	try	my
fly	why	shy	fry	sky

1. Did James ___________ to win the contest or did he just give up?

2. The tot did not ___________ when he fell on the pavement.

3. I hope we can ___________ on a jet to Manhattan.

4. I expect Liz will ___________ the fish.

5. ___________dad is quite upset!

6. The ___________ is red at sunset.

7. The cabin is ___________ a small pond.

8. I think Edwin is___________in class.

9. The ___________salesman sold dad the old junk.

10. ___________are you so sad?

Mark syllable and vowel

Write the word without the final consonants (leave the vowel open). Mark the syllable and vowel.

mĕn c	mē o
him	____________________
sock	____________________
hem	____________________
wet	____________________
got	____________________
shed	____________________
not	____________________
bed	____________________
hop	____________________
met	____________________

Mark the syllables: c = closed; e = v-e; o = open. Mark the vowels long or short. Read the nonsense syllables.

demp	chone	strim
vene	milp	shep
ble	cro	clebe
trine	ope	dru
chy	und	bry

Write the nonsense syllables from above into the correct columns.

closed	**v-e**	**open**
__________	__________	__________
__________	__________	__________
__________	__________	__________
__________	__________	__________
__________	__________	__________

Circle any open syllables. Do not circle <u>to</u> or <u>the</u>. Read the sentence, cover it, and write it on the line. Uncover it and check your spelling.

1. We will fly to Alaska.

____

____

2. Steve will try to go to the game.

____

____

3. I like the springtime so much.

____

____

4. My dad made cupcakes and I frosted them.

____

____

5. Mom will fry fish and make a sandwich.

____

____

Mark all the open syllables in the sentences below. Do not mark to or the). Read the sentences.
e.g. shȳ
o

1. I think that he is shy with my mom.

2. I wish I had my math all done.

3. The student will go take the spelling test.

4. I hope we can go to the basketball game.

5. My Gram went to Wisconsin with us, but she did not like to fly.

6. Dave has the flu so he will be at home.

7. Jake did not cry when he lost the game.

8. The kids have a sly plan.

9. We expect to get this mess up by the time Mom gets home.

10. The sky is so red at sunset!

Combine the first syllable with the second syllable. Write the word on the line. Cover the divided words and read the written words.

be - gin = ______________

pro - gram = ______________

mi - nus = ______________

be - hind = ______________

ba - sic = ______________

jel - lo = ______________

bo - nus = ______________

re - sult = ______________

re - fund = ______________

ban - jo = ______________

de - fend = ______________

tu - lip = ______________

be - ware = ______________

po - lite = ______________

re - quest = ______________

mo - ment = ______________

ro - bot = ______________

re - lax = ______________

o - pen = ______________

si - lent = ______________

Read the syllables on each side of the box. Draw a line to connect syllables to form real words.

stu	lite
pro	tect
po	dent

pre	cret
be	ware
se	pare

ba	nus
mi	ment
mo	sic

do	quest
re	self
my	nate

Write the words above on the lines below. Read the words.

______________________ ______________________

______________________ ______________________

______________________ ______________________

______________________ ______________________

______________________ ______________________

______________________ ______________________

Read the syllables on each side of the box. Draw a line to connect syllables to form real words.

pro	bot
ro	lip
tu	test

de	grate
spo	pend
mi	ken

re	mand
de	ken
bro	tire

sky	line
mo	sult
re	tel

Write the words above on the lines below. Read the words.

Divide each word below into syllables. Read the word. Write the syllables on the lines.

human =_______ _______

program =_______ _______

behave =_______ _______

bonus =_______ _______

silent =_______ _______

hotel =_______ _______

student =_______ _______

locate =_______ _______

begin =_______ _______

frozen =_______ _______

hello =_______ _______

prevent =_______ _______

pupil =_______ _______

require =_______ _______

remind =_______ _______

secret =_______ _______

polite =_______ _______

pretend =_______ _______

female =_______ _______

rodent =_______ _______

Divide each word below into syllables. Read the word. Write the syllables on the lines.

pretend =	______	______	silent =	______	______
relish =	______	______	solid =	______	______
begin =	______	______	cabin =	______	______
topic =	______	______	tulip =	______	______
exit =	______	______	prevent =	______	______

Write the words above into the correct columns below.

first syllable = closed	**first syllable = open**
______________	______________
______________	______________
______________	______________
______________	______________
______________	______________

Read the sentence. Select the correct word from the box to complete the sentence. Write the word on the line. Reread the completed sentence. Use each word in the box only once.

minus	silent	prepare	bonus	robot
label	program	secret	moment	behind

1. Jane had a ___________ to share with all of us.

2. I will dictate a ___________ word on the spelling test.

3. The game must begin this ___________ .

4. The ball is hidden ___________the brick wall.

5. Six ___________ five = *one.*

6. The TV ___________ will begin at nine p.m.

7. The kids wish there was a ___________ to mop up this mess!

8. Mr. Smith demands that the class be ___________.

9. Dad had to ___________ for his long trip.

10. The ___________ got wet and came off this can.

Underline or "scoop" the syllables in the words below. Mark the syllables. Mark vowels long or short. e.g. bē wāre
o v-e

beware	rotate	prepare
female	define	polite
pretend	protect	spoken
request	open	refund
erase	frozen	basic

Rewrite the words on the lines below.

_______________ _______________ _______________

_______________ _______________ _______________

_______________ _______________ _______________

_______________ _______________ _______________

_______________ _______________ _______________

There are words spelled incorrectly in each sentence. They are underlined. Proofread the sentence and add capital letters and punctuation. Rewrite it on the line provided.

1. the lak is frozen and so we can skute

2. you must protekt your sken when you go in the sun

3. the studet depended on his clasmate for help

4. the big contist will begin in a momet

5. mr. jones reqested that kate be silint

Choose a syllable from each box to make a real word on the line above it. Write the word on the line.

1. jel___ = ____________

dy	py	ly

2. ba___ = ____________

dy	by	ly

3. can___ = ____________

ty	my	dy

4. ti___ = ____________

ny	by	fy

5. gra___ = ____________

by	vy	my

6. han___ = ____________

by	try	dy

7. fif___ = ____________

my	ty	gry

8. la___ = ____________

vy	fy	dy

9. emp___ = ____________

ty	ly	zy

10. sil___ = ____________

by	ly	fy

11. la___ = ____________

zy	fy	by

12. na___ = ____________

dy	vy	by

Underline or "scoop" the words into syllables. Read the word. Write the syllables on the lines.

daddy = __________ __________

crazy = __________ __________

Molly = __________ __________

lady = __________ __________

plenty = __________ __________

fifty = __________ __________

silly = __________ __________

gravy = __________ __________

cozy = __________ __________

buggy = __________ __________

funny = __________ __________

Read each sentence. Find words with y at the end. Circle the word then underline or "scoop" and mark the syllables. Rewrite the sentence on the line. Add capital letters and punctuation.

1. jenny will smile if her daddy brings her home a puppy

2. the candy in the pantry is in a handy spot

3. at times, that crazy kid acts like a baby

4. jimmy is in the navy

5. we like molly because she is such a funny lady

Read the sentence. Select the correct word from the box to complete the sentence. Write the word on the line. Reread the completed sentence. Use each word in the box only once.

empty	trolly	fifty
plenty	lady	

1. I think we have _______________ of candy for the kids.

2. I like that _______________ ride but it makes me dizzy.

3. Take the _______________ cans back to the store.

4. There will be _______________ kids in that funny class skit.

5. The _______________ put the pansy in the vase.

Write the words from each sentence that end in y .

1. ________________________ ________________________

2. ________________________ ________________________

3. ________________________

4. ________________________ ________________________

5. ________________________ ________________________

Divide each word below into syllables. Write the syllables on the lines. Mark syllable types.

provide =	______	______	crazy =	______	______
lady =	______	______	puppy =	______	______
invade =	______	______	skyline =	______	______
gravy =	______	______	combine =	______	______
plenty =	______	______	pansy =	______	______

Cover one word at a time and write it in the correct column below. Check spelling.

first syllable = closed	first syllable = open
______________	______________
______________	______________
______________	______________
______________	______________
______________	______________

Read the syllables on each side of the box. Draw a line to connect syllables to form real words.

pen	ly
bel	ty
plen	ny

can	ly
dol	by
ba	dy

hap	py
bun	ty
fif	ny

po	py
la	ny
pup	zy

Write the words above on the lines below. Read the words.

Mark syllable types and vowels. Combine the syllables into words and write them on the lines.

con - so - nant =____________________________

gal - ax - y =____________________________

co - co - nut =____________________________

e - las - tic =____________________________

ed - u - cate =____________________________

e - quip - ment =____________________________

dis - re - spect =____________________________

de - vel - op - ment= ____________________________

vol - ca - no =____________________________

reg - u - late =____________________________

Mark syllable types and vowels. Combine the syllables into words and write them on the lines.

mel - o - dy = ______________________

vi - o - lin = ______________________

u - ten - sil = ______________________

vid - e - o = ______________________

com - pre - hend = ______________________

de - mol - ish = ______________________

re - fresh - ment = ______________________

im - po - lite = ______________________

tux - e - do = ______________________

mi - cro - scope = ______________________

Read the sentence. Select the correct word from the box to complete the sentence. Write the word on the line. Reread the completed sentence. Use each word in the box only once.

equipment	graduate	develop	galaxy	microscopes
elastic	demolish	destructive	coconut	refreshments

1. The child shot an ________________ band at Sally.

2. Bill will __________________ in the spring.

3. Did Tom kick the blocks and ___________________ my *house*?

4. Jenny will plan the ______________________ for the club picnic.

5. The class must share six _______________________ in the lab.

6. The ____________________ is so much fun to study.

7. The old ___________________ is in the shop's basement.

8. The consultant must __________________a plan for the company.

9. I do not like ____________________ in candy.

10. The ___________________ volcano was not expected.

Read the words. Write syllables on the lines. Mark the syllables and rewrite the word.

equipment = _______ _______ _______ ______________________

develop = _______ _______ _______ ______________________

volcano = _______ _______ _______ ______________________

disrespect = _______ _______ _______ ______________________

regulate = _______ _______ _______ ______________________

elastic = _______ _______ _______ ______________________

requirement = _______ _______ _______ ______________________

impolite = _______ _______ _______ ______________________

microscope = _______ _______ _______ ______________________

refreshment = _______ _______ _______ ______________________

coconut = _______ _______ _______ ______________________

Divide multisyllabic words by underlining or "scooping" syllables. Read the sentences.

1. Let's stop here for rest and refreshments.

2. If that volcano explodes, it may be quite destructive.

3. We will get that basketball and go to the game.

4. Jenny was impolite to her dad.

5. Sandy will calculate those math problems.

Write the multisyllabic words on the lines below,

1. ________________

2. ________________ ________________ ________________

3. ________________

4. ________________ ________________

5. ________________ ________________ ________________

Read the words. Circle all the words with an a at the end in an open syllable. Underline or "scoop" syllables. Mark the exceptions.

e.g. (ul tra)

robot	Donna	extra
comma	motel	antenna
umbrella	donate	relax
planet	Edna	Atlanta
pantry	delta	Anna
student	index	skyline
defend	escape	crazy
Calcutta	cupcake	jelly
scuba	magnet	Emma
crazy	secret	vanilla

Read the syllables on each side of the box. Draw a line to connect syllables to form real words.

a	maze
um	ty
plen	pire

com	pete
a	take
mis	woke

pro	tect
com	while
a	ma

ex	sist
a	lone
in	tra

Write the words above on the lines below. Read the words.

Add a as the first syllable to each word below. Mark the a with a ə to indicate sound. Write the word on the line. Read the words.

__live =______________

__bility =______________

__side =______________

__muse =______________

__go =______________

__long =______________

__wake =______________

__woke =______________

__lone =______________

__laska =______________

__maze =______________

Write three sentences using at least one word above in each sentence. Proofread carefully.

1.____

____

2.____

____

3.____

____

Read the sentence. Select the correct word from the box to complete the sentence. Write the word on the line. Reread the completed sentence. Use each word in the box only once.

along	Alaska	adopt	amuse	ago
awhile	alive	alone	awaken	extra

1. Long ____________ , Jane met Bill at the baseball game.

2. I like to ____________ the children with jokes.

3. ____________ is an extremely cold state!

4. I will try to find a wild rose____________ the path.

5. Mr. and Mrs. Jones want to ____________ a child so much!

6. Can I have this ____________ cake?

7. Be careful not to ____________ the baby.

8. You must rest for ____________ .

9. The puppy was hit by the van but it is still ____________ .

10. Do not go to the mall ____________ .

Circle the syllable with the exception to the open syllable. Write the syllables on the lines. Combine the syllables into words and write them on the lines.

pres - i - dent = ______ ______ ______ ________________

com - pli - ment = ______ ______ ______ ________________

con - fi - dent = ______ ______ ______ ________________

cav - i - ty = ______ ______ ______ ________________

cab - i - net = ______ ______ ______ ________________

sub-sti-tute = ______ ______ ______ ________________

an-i-mal = ______ ______ ______ ________________

im-i-tate = ______ ______ ______ ________________

sen-si-tive = ______ ______ ______ ________________

Es-ki-mo = ______ ______ ______ ________________

Find and circle the unaccented open syllable words. Some will have a at the beginning, some will have a at the end, and others will have i in the middle of a word. Underline the syllables. Mark the syllables and the vowels. Read the sentences.

1. Donna will finish the job in a year.

2. Sandra thinks this math problem is difficult.

3. Brenda went to Alaska a long time ago.

4. Beth's sensitive skin broke *out* in a rash.

5 The state of Alaska has lots of frozen tundra.

6. Did that trick amaze the class?

7. Sandra likes to go to the festival.

8. Rosa is the class president.

9. We have had a substitute in class *now* for quite awhile.

10. Kendra had to go to the hospital.

Vocabulary Practice:
Create sentences that include the vocabulary words below. Use a dictionary or electronic spell checker as needed. Underline or "scoop" each syllable in the vocabulary words.

5.2	5.3	5.4	5.5
locate	plenty	regulate	aside
provide	grumpy	develop	amaze
depend	lazy	impolite	alone
protect	empty	equipment	amuse
donate	angry	demolish	extra
predict		refreshment	alive
defend			hesitate
request			compliment
demand			festival
			confident

Story Starter:
At the end of Step 5 create a story that includes many (at least 5) of the vocabulary words below. This story is about the future. Underline each vocabulary word used from the list below.

robots	demand	extra	expensive
request	plenty	alive	thrill
provide	handy	amazement	shops
students	development	locate	jobs
program	demolish	compare	find

5A

Student Workbook
Five A

ISBN 1-56778-086-5

Wilson Language Training
175 West Main Street
Millbury, Massachusetts 01527-1441
(508) 865-5699